Original title:
Botanical Bliss

Copyright © 2025 Creative Arts Management OÜ
All rights reserved.

Author: Harrison Blake
ISBN HARDBACK: 978-1-80566-791-9
ISBN PAPERBACK: 978-1-80566-811-4

Nature's Gentle Palette

In gardens bright with crazy hues,
The flowers wear their sparkly shoes.
A daffodil just danced a jig,
While roses giggle, oh so big.

The daisies play a game of tag,
While tulips strut in quite a brag.
Each petal's painted with delight,
Making nature feel so right.

Fragrant Reverie

A mint leaf twirls upon the breeze,
While thyme sings songs among the trees.
The daisies chat about the sun,
Saying, 'Aren't we just so fun?'

Lavender's scent floats like a dream,
As bees buzz by in giggling gleam.
The rosemary's got tales to tell,
Of baking treats that turned out well.

Echoes of the Forest

In the woods where mushrooms moan,
Squirrels fight for acorns grown.
The ferns are gossiping with ease,
While tree trunks hug the bumblebees.

A wise old owl wears specs so round,
He critiques the rabbits all around.
Nature chuckles, what a hoot,
With every hop and every root.

Dance of the Daisies

The daisies twirl in afternoon,
Wearing crowns of golden bloom.
With every step, they laugh and sway,
Chasing worries far away.

A butterfly joins in the cheer,
With a flutter that draws near.
Together they pirouette and prance,
In the sun, they take a chance.

Feast of the Foliage

In the garden, greens abound,
Lettuce giggles, growing round.
Tomatoes waltz, they spin with glee,
Carrots hide, oh what a spree!

Radishes are dressed in reds,
While broccoli shares its heads.
Spinach dons a leafy crown,
As peas roll by, they twirl around.

The Allure of Orchids

Orchids pout in shades so bright,
Dancing in the morning light.
Their petals tease with playful flair,
Whispering secrets in the air.

Some flirt with spots, others stripes,
Each one schemes with leafy types.
They giggle soft, their colors clash,
In a game of floral flash.

A Lullaby of Lavender

Lavender waves, like ocean tides,
In fields where sleepy sunshine hides.
Buzzing bees hum lullabies,
While snoozing blooms wear sleepy sighs.

Fragrant dreams in violet hues,
Dancing away the daytime blues.
Whispering thoughts of honeyed nights,
As day drifts off, and moon ignites.

Blossom's Soliloquy

Blossoms converse, with petals wide,
"Watch me sway," one says with pride.
"Oh please," laughs a daisy near,
"Your dance is nice, but mine is sheer!"

Sunflowers rise, with heads held high,
Plotting schemes as clouds drift by.
"Let's paint the sky," one flower beams,
As they all bask in floral dreams.

Where the Wildflowers Grow

In fields where daisies may just trip,
A clumsy bee takes a wild dip.
Giggling tulips wave with glee,
Saying, "Look at that bee, oh dear!"

Amid the clover, grasshoppers dance,
While workaholic ants miss their chance.
"Hey, slow down! Enjoy the show!"
But off they march, never too slow.

Sunflowers turn to catch a glance,
Of clouds that float like a bad romance.
"Hey, couple clouds, don't be so shy!"
They puff and drift, just passing by.

So in this patch of colors bright,
Even the weeds know how to kite.
With laughter bubbling in the air,
Nature's jesters have joy to share.

The Joy of Greenery

Leaves are whispering silly things,
As squirrels perform on tree branch swings.
"Don't call me nutty!" one squirrel cries,
Dodging acorns with practiced highs.

Ferns make hats for passing snails,
While roots debate over happy tales.
"Is water rare, or am I dry?"
They laugh as raindrops plop and sigh.

Moss cushions the feet of frogs who leap,
Wishing each splash was a joke so deep.
"Ribbit! Did you hear my last great pun?"
The pond erupts; who knew it'd run?

In gardens where greens can be loud,
Giggles float behind every cloud.
Nature's chuckle, a delightful tease,
Turns every plant into parties, with ease.

Nature's Color Symphony

Bees in bow ties zipping about,
Compose sweet tunes with joyful shout.
"Buzzing along! What's next on stage?"
A poppy replies, "Let's steal the page!"

The daisies play their trumpet tune,
While lilacs groove with a scented swoon.
"Hey, you over there! Swing that stem!"
Nature nods; it's a grand diadem.

The roses boast their vibrant hues,
While violets grin with morning dew.
Sassy petals wink and sway,
Creating rhythms throughout the day.

In the chorus of blooms so bright,
Color clashes cause a comic fright.
Yet nature laughs, in jest it flows,
A symphony where humor grows.

Garden of Whimsy

In my garden, the gnomes have a chat,
Discussing if worms make better hats.
"Mine's a classic, looks great!" says Fred,
"Worms just squirm… it's like wearing bread!"

The sunflowers plot a funny dance,
While roses roll their eyes at chance.
"Why the long stems?" they sigh and whine,
"Just once, we'll reach the sun, oh divine!"

Busy bees wear striped pajamas,
As ladybugs chant their little dramas.
"Why can't we catch a break?" they plead,
As butterflies flutter with laughter to lead.

In this garden where jokes are spry,
Even the weeds wonder why.
Humor blossoms in every nook,
Join the joy with nature's book!

Verdant Reverie

In a garden so wild, a frog starts to dance,
With daisies and dandelions, taken a chance.
He hops and he skips, showing off his flair,
While butterflies giggle, floating in the air.

Lettuce joined in, all dressed in his best,
Said, "Kale, keep it cool, let's not be a pest!"
But spinach just grinned, munching leaves with glee,
As carrots yelled, "Hey! We're root vegetables, you see!"

The Language of Leaves

A maple leaf spoke with a voice quite absurd,
"I'd leaf it alone, but I'm feeling quite stirred!"
While ferns whispered secrets, green jokes to the sun,
Saying, "Photosynthesis? Now that's some fun!"

A tulip chimed in, with a story to tell,
"Why don't trees ever play hide and seek well?"
The answer, of course, a laugh in disguise,
"Because they always get spotted!" oh how time flies!

Sunlit Petals

Under sun's warm glow, the flowers compete,
For the title of brightest, who's sweet and who's neat.
A rose threw a tantrum, all prickly and red,
As daisies just laughed, "Oh, lighten up, Fred!"

With sunflowers tall, showing off their tall height,
They waved to the clouds, "Come join in our flight!"
But clouds just rolled by, with a grin on their face,
Sprinkling a shower, a floral embrace!

A Symphony of Stems

In a garden of stems, the orchestra starts,
With each leafy green, they're playing their parts.
A trumpet from tulips, so bold and so bright,
While thorns play the drums, in a wild, prickly fright.

Violets sing soft, a sweet, gentle tune,
As the wind joins in, whistling over the moon.
A concert of color, laughter alight,
With every bloom dancing, what a joyful sight!

Blooming Whimsy

In gardens where the daisies dance,
The tulips wear a silly stance.
A rogue fern tries to steal the show,
While sunflowers giggle, row by row.

A carrot's joke makes onions cry,
As broccoli dreams of flying high.
The peas insist on winning the race,
But the sprouts just smile, they love the chase.

A cactus jokes with flowers bright,
"Why bloom so close to buzzing fright?"
Yet bumblebees hum, full of glee,
Sipping nectar, they tease the bee.

So let's toast to this leafy spree,
Where plants unite in pure glee.
With roots that wiggle and leaves that sway,
In this garden, we laugh all day.

Ephemeral Eden

In a patch where thyme plays peekaboo,
   Mint is munching on morning dew.
   The wildflowers sport quirky hats,
While beetles throw gardening spats.

   Robins recite the best of puns,
   As daisies plot gardening runs.
  A dandelion squeaks, "I'm a star!"
While grasshoppers argue who's bizarre.

A plant named Fern feels quite elite,
   Telling tales of roots bittersweet.
The violets crack jokes, soft and flimsy,
While mushrooms chuckle, feeling whimsy.

So here in this transient realm we play,
Where petals flutter, and frolic all day.
Life is a garden filled with applause,
  In this spot, we're bound by no laws.

Verdant Whispers

In the wood where the wild things cheer,
There's a whispering leaf with a secret to share.
A squirrel chuckles at acorn dreams,
While blossoms bloom with playful schemes.

The posies giggle at a bee's buzz,
While branches sway, giving hugs just because.
"A pot of soil is where I belong!"
Chortles a clover, crafting a song.

A vine tells tales with a twist and a shout,
Of kale trying out for a chef's outing, no doubt.
Wandering stems with shoes made of lace,
Sashay among the greens as if in a race.

Come join these whispers, light and bright,
In this garden of joy, let's take flight.
With laughter sprouting from every nook,
Every petal's surprise, a fun little book.

Petals of Serenity

Amidst the roses, a tulip grins wide,
Wearing a funny, bright orange tide.
A daffodil dances with no care at all,
While violets compete in a colorball.

The ferns gossip about sun's warm glow,
"Did you see the way the daisies grow?"
A lily sighs, "I need a stand!"
As daisies whisper, "We're all quite grand!"

A wildflower cries, "I lost my hat!",
And the bumblebees tease, "You look fine, just fat!"
Petals flutter with laughter, a joyous spree,
Every sprout knows how fun it can be.

So let's gather here, where laughter's the creed,
With every bloom, we plant a new seed.
In this patch of joy where whimsy delights,
Life unfurls softly with giggles and sights.

Serenity in the Succulents

In pots so small, they barely fit,
Cacti wear hats, looking quite lit.
Succulents dance in the morning sun,
Spinning tales of a life that's fun.

With roots so deep, they hold their ground,
While others flail, they spin around.
Sharing smiles and sunshine gleams,
They whisper secrets of tropical dreams.

Reflections Among the Roses

Roses giggle beneath the stars,
Mumbling softly about their scars.
One loves blue, another loves red,
They blossom tales of love and bread.

With thorns on guard, they play pretend,
"Don't touch!" they cry, "We're not your friend!"
But sniff them close, they scent the night,
Filling hearts with pure delight.

The Enchantment of Ferns

Ferns like to dance in a shady breeze,
Whispering jokes, their laughter's a tease.
"Why don't we tell a few tall tales?"
They sway and giggle, their joy prevails.

Spreading out like a fluffy hairdo,
They jive along with the morning dew.
When sunlight fades, they huddle tight,
Dreaming of mischief throughout the night.

Under the Canopy of Life

Underneath leaves, the chatter grows,
Trees gossip about the garden shows.
Frogs on a log strike a funny pose,
While dancing ants steal all the clothes.

Beneath the arch of leafy dreams,
Creatures plot with zany schemes.
Nature's circus, wild and free,
Tickles the roots of you and me.

Symphony of Green

In the garden, plants do dance,
Wiggling leaves in a joyful prance.
Tulips giggle, daisies snicker,
Sunflowers sway, 'Hey, look at her!'

Bees are buzzing a silly tune,
Wearing tiny hats under the moon.
While the carrots argue with the peas,
'I'm more orange!' 'No, I'm the tease!'

A raucous choir of greens and blooms,
Frolicking sounds in garden rooms.
Even weeds can't help but laugh,
As they form their own silly gaffe.

In this patch where laughter grows,
Every plant is one that knows:
Life's too short for a frown or sigh,
So let's plant joy and reach the sky!

The Garden's Embrace

In the garden's warm, sweet hug,
Roses joke with every bug.
Lettuce thinks it's quite the clown,
Waving leaves like a leafy gown.

Tomatoes roll under the sun,
While radishes have a frosty fun.
Beans climb high, shout with glee,
'Look at me, I'm a leafy tree!'

Sunset hues paint the sky,
The garden whispers, 'Oh my, oh my!'
Petunias gossip with cucumber vines,
Sharing secrets with winks and signs.

Let's raise a glass, a plant parade,
To all the laughs that life has made.
In every bloom, a tale of cheer,
A garden's heart is ever near!

Secrets in the Soil

They say the dirt holds tales untold,
Of love and laughter, brave and bold.
Worms throw parties, so much fun,
Dirt baths underneath the sun.

With roots that wriggle, secrets blend,
Every sprout has a story to send.
Carrots play hide and seek with corn,
"Oh where's my friend? Don't be forlorn!"

Underneath, a raucous glee,
Where every seed dreams to be free.
Moles are DJs, spinning tunes,
As cabbages dance beneath the moons.

So dig deep down, don't just scratch,
You'll find that soil is quite the catch.
Each clump and crumb a chuckle brings,
A lively world where laughter sings!

Blooming Dreams

In a patch of dreams, colors collide,
Petals giggle, swaying with pride.
A daffodil shouts, 'I'm the best!'
While violets boast, 'We're all the jest!'

Butterflies skip like little kids,
While tulips cheer and do the bids.
Every bud has a quirky dream,
To sprout up high and make the scene.

Even the thorns join in the fun,
Saying, 'We can shine, we can run!'
In this world of vibrant schemes,
Laughter echoes through blooming dreams.

So come and join the floral spree,
Where petals frolic wild and free.
Each burst of color, a laugh divine,
In the garden where joy will shine!

Floral Mosaic

Petals giggle in the breeze,
Colors jive with such great ease.
Dandelions dance, a wild ballet,
While roses blush at the bouquet.

Bees in bow ties buzz with flair,
Sipping nectar everywhere.
Sunflowers strut, tall and bright,
In their hats made of pure sunlight.

Cacti strike a pose so bold,
Spiking jokes never grow old.
Tulips tease the daffodils,
With puns that give them all great thrills.

In this patchwork of flower power,
Laughter blooms in every hour.
Join the fun, don't be a bore,
In this garden, there's so much more!

Entwined in Eden

Two vines waltz on a smoky vine,
Twirling leaves, oh how they shine!
With roots like legs in a tangled race,
They giggle soft, a leafy embrace.

Lettuce laughs, "I'm not a rom-com!"
While carrots joke, "I'm the real bomb!"
Intertwined, they sway with grace,
A salad toss, a fun embrace.

Morning glories climb with zest,
"Can you beat my bloom?" they jest.
Violets smirk from the garden floor,
"Let's open up and explore!"

In this Eden filled with glee,
Every petal's a joke for free.
Come join this merry, leafy game,
In this paradise, fun is the aim!

A Canopy of Color

Underneath this vibrant dome,
Colors clash, but feel like home.
Leaves are chattering, oh so loud,
A rainbow's here, and it's quite proud.

Fronds wave in the sunny air,
Telling tales without a care.
"Hey, look at me, I'm bright and bold!"
"Yeah, but I'm the one who won't grow old!"

Orchids giggle, "Let's play dress-up!"
While daisies sip from a teacup.
"Shady, shady, don't be shy!"
Colors laugh as clouds drift by.

This canopy, a lively shard,
Where every plant is a quirky bard.
Join this party, bring your zest,
Under this roof, you'll feel your best!

Whispers Through the Vines

Whispers float on a viney breeze,
"Did you hear what the daisy sees?"
Snippets of gossip, oh so sweet,
"Come closer, friend, take a seat!"

"Roses said they're tired of fame,
Daisies rolling their eyes at the game."
"Sunflowers strut, do they ever sleep?"
"Who knows, but their secrets we'll keep."

The ferns are giggling, leaf to leaf,
"A ferny fairy's quite the thief!"
"Beware of bees with sticky plans,
They'll buzz you into their flower bands!"

Through the vines, the laughter flows,
As petals share their playful prose.
Join the whispers, take a chance,
In this garden, let's dance and prance!

Garden of Delights

In the garden, gnomes do dance,
Wearing hats that make no sense.
Veggies gossip, flowers snicker,
While the weeds just grow thicker.

The tomatoes sing in red parade,
Cucumbers wearing a leafy braid.
Radishes play hide and seek,
With a shy little turnip feeling meek.

Carrots tell jokes in rows so neat,
While insects share a tasty treat.
Bees buzz loud with joyous glee,
As daisies sway, oh can't you see?

In this patch, fun is the key,
Nature's circus, wild and free.
Each plant has its part to play,
What a nutty, leafy day!

Green Secrets Unveiled

The lilacs whisper tales of spring,
While lazy slugs plot everything.
Hidden secrets behind each leaf,
Like who's the loudest, to their relief.

The ferns are shy, they fold and bend,
While daisies giggle at every end.
An old oak tree gives wise advice,
"Life's a garden, roll the dice!"

The sunflowers wear shades, feeling cool,
As the cacti join, breaking the rule.
They poke fun at every passerby,
"You bring the snacks, we'll reach the sky!"

Glimpses of glee in every nook,
In this green realm, come take a look!
Nature's chorus sings so bright,
In this secret garden, pure delight.

The Elegance of Earth

Oh, the earth dresses up in hue,
With plants that flaunt their vibrant view.
Lavender laughs, "Aren't I divine?"
While dandelions call, "Let's all intertwine!"

The soil hums with a jazzy beat,
As worms do cha-cha under your feet.
Mushrooms strut in an elegant way,
Saying, "Join us for a shroomy fête!"

Petunias pose, demanding a show,
While violets whisper secrets low.
The daisies roll eyes, oh what a sight,
As nature's ball shines ever so bright.

In the garden, elegance thrives,
With quirks of green, laughter arrives.
Each plant a character, lively and spry,
In this earthy play, oh my, oh my!

Symphony of the Soil

Gather 'round, let's hear the tune,
Of earthworms in a wiggly swoon.
Grasses sway in rhythmic delight,
While pebbles drum all through the night.

The daisies clap with petals wide,
While crickets chirp, a band to guide.
Frogs croak loud, a bass so deep,
As the moon winks down to peek.

Cabbages hum a mellow song,
As butterflies twirl, twirling along.
The marigolds wink with a bright cheer,
Welcoming springtime, oh so dear!

Soil's the stage, nature's the band,
With rhythms that take you by hand.
Laughter and bloom fill every hole,
Join this joyful, earthy stroll!

Tapestry of Leaves

In the garden, a leaf took flight,
Hitching rides on a dog's tail, what a sight!
It dived and twirled, oh what a dance,
As the dog paused, it lost its chance.

A squirrel chuckled high up in the tree,
Watching the leaf, so wild and free.
It yelled out, "Hey! That's quite a trip!"
While munching nuts, it took a sip.

The sun peeked through like a curious spy,
As the leaf made friends with a dragonfly.
They laughed and joked under skies so blue,
"Who knew leaves could have such a view?"

In this garden, each day's a surprise,
Where laughter blooms in green disguise.
So join the fun, don't be a bore,
With whimsical leaves, let's explore more!

Blossoms in the Breeze

Blossoms giggle as they sway,
Telling secrets in a breezy play.
One said, "I'm pink, and quite a tease!"
The yellow bloom spurted, "I'm here to please!"

A bee buzzed in, quite out of breath,
"Nice to meet you, stop with the jest!"
The blooms erupted in laughter bright,
"Join our fun, it feels so right!"

A dandelion snickered with glee,
"Blow me away and set me free!"
So a gust came and gave it a shove,
Off it twirled, feeling the love.

In the breeze, blossoms spin 'round,
Creating joy on this merry ground.
Laughter flows as fragrances greet,
In this garden, life's oh-so sweet!

Tranquil Vines

Vines on the trellis twirl and sway,
Whispering jokes in a leafy ballet.
One vine joked, "I'm tangled with style!"
While another chimed in, "Stay a while!"

A passerby stumbled, eyes wide with shock,
As a vine tickled him, what a mock!
He giggled and fell in a heap of glee,
"Who knew that plants could play with me?"

Onlookers laughed, giving a cheer,
As playful vines drew everyone near.
One vine stretched high, it loved to tease,
"Think you can catch me? Oh, please!"

In the garden's midst, silliness thrives,
With each green twist, laughter arrives.
Nature's whimsy, a viney delight,
Bringing joy from day to night!

Sunlit Canopy

Under the shade of a leafy dome,
A sunlit canopy feels like home.
A leaf fell down, landing like grace,
"I'm here for the party, what a nice place!"

A chipmunk arrived, all dressed in brown,
With acorn hats, he didn't frown.
He tapped his feet, made a leafy stage,
While the flowers giggled in a blooming rage.

The sunbeams danced through the leafy maze,
Lighting up laughter in playful haze.
"Let's throw a ball!" shouted a bright tulip,
"In this sunshine, we'll all take a trip!"

So, they all twirled in the golden glow,
Playing all day, feeling the flow.
In the sunlit canopy, joy's the decree,
Where nature and fun, go hand in hand, you see!

Foliage Fantasia

In the garden where veggies play,
Carrots wear hats, it's quite a display.
Beets bust out laughing in rows not so neat,
While lettuce does yoga, it's hard to compete.

Tomatoes play hide and seek in the dirt,
Peppers write poetry, oh how they flirt!
Cucumbers gossip, it's a real hoot,
As radishes dance in comical suit.

Nectar's Embrace

Bees in bow ties, oh what a sight,
Swirling 'round flowers from morning till night.
Buzzing their tunes in synchronized glee,
Honeycomb parties, it's quite the jamboree!

Butterflies giggle, fluttering by,
Whispering secrets while sipping on thyme.
A nectar-filled punch with a splash of delight,
Laughing 'til dusk, what a magical night!

Fragrant Serenade

Lavender sings in the warm summer breeze,
Rosemary cracks jokes, sends you to your knees.
Thyme tells tall tales of days long ago,
While sage gives a wink, putting on a show.

Jasmine draped jewels in the soft moonlight,
Lemon balm giggles, 'Oh, this feels just right!'
A bouquet of laughter floats through the air,
In this merry garden, free from all care.

The Dance of Daisies

Daisies don tutus, twirling with grace,
In a floral ballet, they claim the best space.
Sunflowers cheer, waving their big heads,
While violets chuckle, lying down in their beds.

Pansies perform in a colorful riot,
Oh, how they leap! It's a wild plant diet.
With roots in the rhythm, they sway and they spin,
Celebrating life in this garden of whim.

The Language of Flowers

Roses whisper jokes in bloom,
Daisies giggle, making room.
Tulips dance with a silly sway,
While violets blush at what they say.

Sunflowers nod, they know it all,
Chasing bees in a floral ball.
Petunias tease with colorful cheer,
"Come join the fun, the party's here!"

Lilies laugh when guests arrive,
Their fragrance makes all spirits thrive.
Pansies wink with a playful smile,
"Stay for tea, we'll chat a while!"

In the garden, humor grows,
Nature's chuckles, as everyone knows.
A floral pun, a cheeky jest,
In the patch of blooms, we are blessed.

Awakened Roots

Roots are grumpy, tangled tight,
"Why can't we see the sun's bright light?"
They mumble low, with whispers loud,
"Can we not join the leafy crowd?"

Sprouts pop up with a cheeky giggle,
"Stretch your legs! Just learn to wiggle!"
Buds break out in raucous laughter,
"Join the dance, discover the rafter!"

Worms throw party hats underground,
"You haven't lived until you've drowned!"
In rainbows of dirt, they have their fun,
Belly laughs till the rising sun.

A garden's roots with a sense of play,
Finding joy in the earth's ballet.
Awakened from their sleepy snooze,
They'll trade their blues for happier hues.

Harmony in the Hedges

The hedges gossip in a hush,
"Did you see that last week's bush?"
They share secrets, oh so sly,
"Daffodils dressed up to fly!"

A ladybug gave quite the show,
With a lady's twirl, oh so slow.
She charmed the blooms, oh what a feat,
While daisies jived to the beetle's beat!

Thistles prick their ears with glee,
"Nobody likes a thorny spree!"
Yet they laugh and poke their jokes,
As the garden bursts with leafy folks.

In tangled green where flowers meet,
The hedges sway to their own beat.
A symphony of giggles, loud and bright,
Where nature's laughter fills the night.

Raindrops on Lilies

Raindrops roll on lily pads,
"Look out here, it's time for jabs!"
Splashing fun like kids at play,
"Catch me quick, I'm on my way!"

They twirl and spin, they slide and fall,
A watery dance, they heed the call.
"Shower us with giggles, please!"
As droplets dance with the gentle breeze.

Petals open wide with flair,
"Look at us, we don't have a care!"
While frogs croak jokes from the side,
"Come join the splash, we'll take a ride!"

With smiles bright as morning dew,
Nature sings, a joy so true.
Raindrops fall in rhythmic bounce,
A wet and wild floral pounce!

Serenade of the Sunflower

In fields where sunflowers sway so bright,
They nod their heads, oh what a sight!
Their yellow crowns a sunny glare,
They dance to breezes, without a care.

Bees buzz around like little cars,
While squirrels compete for nature's bars.
A sunflower smiles, but who can tell?
If it prefers sunshine or wishes well?

Their petals spread, a wide embrace,
Yet they can't help but flaunt their grace.
With roots so deep, they grow so proud,
Taking selfies; they'd draw a crowd!

So here's to blooms with silly names,
Who play in sunlight, like silly games.
With puns and pouts, they rule the day,
In this funny flower ballet!

The Dance of Decay

Leaves fall down like nature's confetti,
While worms in the soil make themselves ready.
The trees hold on, their limbs all askew,
Embracing the breeze, waving adieu.

Mushrooms pop up like guests uninvited,
In the shadiest spots, they get excited.
A squirrel finds treasure, lost and found,
In a pile of leaves, it jumps around!

Pumpkins once proud, now squishy and soft,
Run from the garden, the wind blowing oft.
But not all is sad; it's seasonal fun,
With ghouls and goblins embracing the sun!

So gather your laughter and let it decay,
For every goodbye, there's a new way to play.
With composting jokes, we'll grow and we'll change,
In this dance of decay, we'll never feel strange!

Essence of the Evergreen

Pines stand tall, all dressed in green,
In a winter coat, they reign supreme.
They point to the sky with elegant flair,
Whispering secrets to the crisp, cold air.

Tiny pine cones fall with a clatter,
Spilling their seeds, that's what's the matter.
Squirrels gather them for winter's feast,
Claiming their treasures, their love increased!

Boughs dripping snow in a comical way,
As kids climb up for a snowy play.
Evergreen laughter fills up the woods,
While everyone's busy practicing 'good' moods.

So here's to the trees, the evergreen kind,
With stories to share, that tickle your mind.
In nature's own theater, they take the stage,
Creating humor that never grows age!

Elysium of Eden

In a garden where giggles and blooms collide,
The flowers tell jokes, with petals as pride.
Roses blush red from all the fun,
While daisies spin tales under the sun.

Veggies gossip in rows, what a sight!
With carrots and peas having a light bite.
"Hey there, tomato, you're looking quite ripe!"
"Thanks for the compliment; swing by for a pipe!"

Butterflies flit, in colors so bright,
They dance with the bees, sharing delight.
Tulips tease tulips, 'Oh, you're too tall!"
In this Eden of laughter, there's room for us all.

So come join the party, unleash your zest,
With petals and puns, let nature be blessed.
In this heavenly place where joy takes flight,
We'll hum together until the stars light!

The Garden's Heartbeat

In the garden, ants parade,
Stealing crumbs, but unafraid.
Bees buzz by with playful dance,
While daisies giggle, given a chance.

Sunflowers wear their sunny hats,
Swaying gently, just like cats.
Petunias whisper juicy jokes,
While carrots laugh at silly croaks.

Roses pout when weeds come near,
But then they smirk, with naught a fear.
The melody of rustling leaves,
Cracks me up, my heart believes.

In this realm of greens and shades,
The world's a stage, where fun cascades.
With roots that tickle, grass that sings,
The garden's heart is full of things.

Treasures of the Underbrush

Beneath the ferns, the secrets lie,
With mushrooms wearing caps so spry.
A snail recites its daily grind,
While leafhoppers just laugh behind.

Twigs are thrones for ants at play,
As critters weave their grand ballet.
A spider spins a web so grand,
Declaring, "Look! A house so planned!"

The berries blush, avoiding eyes,
While fireflies twinkle, oh so sly.
The underbrush is filled with cheer,
Where treasures thrive, and fun is near.

In shadows deep, the giggles swell,
As crickets tell their tales so well.
Amongst the roots, where chaos reigns,
Life's little quirks bring joyful gains.

A Floral Odyssey

Petals sail on breezy seas,
Laughing softly with the trees.
Butterflies don their fanciest wear,
While bees hold races in the air.

A tulip trips on morning dew,
Spilling secrets to the crew.
The violets roll in grassy bliss,
Chasing dreams with every whiff.

Sunsets brush the blooms with gold,
Telling stories yet untold.
With each new day, the flowers sing,
In this realm, joy is the king.

The daisies tease the unfolds,
While poppies dare the sun to hold.
What a ride, this floral tale,
In every petal, laughter sails.

Nature's Quietude

In the quiet, mischief stirs,
Nature's charm, like waltzing furs.
Squirrels scamper, ears held high,
Chasing shadows, oh my, oh my!

The rocks giggle, serene and wise,
As lichen whispers, "What a surprise!"
A gentle breeze shakes laughter free,
Dancing wild among the trees.

Mossy carpets invite a nap,
Where dreams bloom within nature's lap.
Each rustle hints at quirky fun,
Even stones play—oh, what a run!

In tranquil moments, laughter grows,
With every leaf, a secret glows.
Nature's quietude wears a grin,
In this stillness, we begin.

Seasonal Journeys

In spring, I sneeze at blooms so bright,
The pollen dances, what a sight!
I trip on grass, I laugh, I roll,
Nature's merry pranksters take their toll.

Summer sun brings bees so bold,
They buzz my ear, I feel so old.
With lemonade in hand, I shout,
'More flowers, please! I'm in no doubt!'

Autumn leaves fall like confetti,
I chase the colors, feeling petty.
With pumpkins round, I paint a grin,
Why did I think I'd never win?

Winter stirs when snowflakes dance,
With frosty breath, I take a chance.
In gardens laid beneath the snow,
I plot and scheme for spring's warm glow.

The Flicker of Fireflies

Little lights blink in the night,
Fireflies play like stars in flight.
I chase and stumble, what a sight,
While frogs are croaking, feeling right.

They flicker here, they flicker there,
I trip on roots, fall in a chair.
With jars in hand, I make a plan,
To catch the glow with little man!

They tease my hair, I swear they plot,
My tangled locks, they like a lot!
But when they land, they simply dance,
And leave me with a funny chance.

So off I go, with laughter loud,
Chasing light amidst the crowd.
A firefly flash is just my style,
I'll smile all night, it's worth the while!

Passages through Petals

Through petals soft as clouds of cream,
I wander lost in flower's dream.
With bees that buzz and colors bright,
I try to dance, I lose my sight.

A daisy calls, 'Come smell my charm!',
I lean too close, I mean no harm.
But my nose gets stuck; oh dear, oh wow!
Next thing I know, I'm taking a bow!

Roses tease with thorns so sly,
I tiptoe 'round, I wave goodbye.
With every step, I laugh and trip,
Flowers giggle, I lose my grip!

Yet as I stroll, I can't resist,
A flower crown I can't dismiss.
I wear it proud, I sing and sway,
In petals' realm, I'll blissfully stay!

Enchanted Earth

When mushrooms pop with spots so bright,
I ponder if they're out for bite.
I crouch to peek, they look so cute,
Next thing I know, I've lost my boot!

The earthworms wiggle, looking sly,
They laugh at me—I can't deny.
With mud on my face and twigs in hair,
It's evident: I shouldn't dare!

The plants all whisper secrets told,
'You'll find treasures, be brave, be bold!'
I search for gold, but here's a snag,
I find instead a wrinkled rag.

Yet still I grin, for what's a find?
In nature's hugs, I'm rarely blind.
With laughter echoing through the ground,
I'm enchanted here; joy is found!

The Essence of Eden

In a garden so bright, where the weeds love to play,
The daisies dance wildly, they sway and they sway.
The roses complain, 'We're just here for the show!'
While the snails plot their heist, moving oh so slow.

With gardener's gloves, they dig for the gold,
But find only worms that are slimy and bold.
The carrots keep laughing, they grow down below,
While radishes giggle, 'We're flushing aglow!'

The sunflowers tower, they sense their own fame,
Yet doubt their own height, is it all just a game?
The bees buzz in circles, a comic charade,
As they sip from the blossoms, their heads in a daze.

Will the weeds take the prize? Only time will reveal,
In this humorous garden, where everything's real.
With joy and with laughter, they all find a way,
To bloom in the chaos, and enjoy every day.

Joy of the Junipers

Oh, the junipers chuckle, with needles so spry,
They poke at the gardeners who pass wandering by.
They argue with cacti, who think they're the best,
It's a prickly affair, just a spiky jest.

The sagebrush is sassy, with a voice like a breeze,
'These junipers think they are so hard to tease!'
But junipers wink, as they bask in the sun,
They're laughing it up, 'Yes, we're all here for fun!'

The pines drop their cones, a hilarious rain,
The cactus starts laughing, and they all feel no pain.
They play leapfrog with shadows, and roll on the floor,
In a world of green giggles, who could ask for more?

So listen dear friend, as you wander this way,
The junipers tell tales that brighten the day.
With each little poke, there's a story to tell,
In this jesting green paradise, all's going quite well.

Wandering through Wilds

In the heart of the wilds, where the foliage plays,
A squirrel tells secrets in shadowy ways.
'The leaves are all gossiping,' he chimes with delight,
As the raccoons snicker and prepare for the night.

The ferns flaunt their fronds, they twist with some flair,
'They're trying to outshine us, but we just don't care!'
The thorns keep their silence, though they lurk in the wings,
While the owls hoot 'round about, to hear what it brings.

In mossy green blankets, the critters do nap,
While crickets write sonnets—beautiful rap!
The flowers throw parties in the cool evening shade,
Charmers in the wild, where friendships are made.

So roam through these wilds, with laughter and cheer,
For in each little rustle, a smile will appear.
The flora and fauna all join in the jest,
In this lively green playground, they're feeling the best.

In the Shade of Giants

Under canopies vast, where the shadows are deep,
The tallest trees whisper, while small critters sleep.
The acorns are plotting a grand little scheme,
While the leaves tease the branches, 'You're losing your gleam!'

The squirrels are acrobats, swinging with glee,
They race up the trunks, the champions of spree.
While mushrooms hold parties, all decked out in cheer,
With fungi on trumpets, they pull crowds from near.

The ferns wear their frond hats, in colors so bright,
Dancing in circles, they twirl with delight.
While the gnarled old roots keep a watchful old eye,
Secretly giggling, 'We're all spry, oh my!'

So come take a seat, in this shade full of fun,
Where laughter is growing, like leaves in the sun.
With whispers of nature, and antics galore,
In the shade of the giants, you'll find laughter more!

The Art of Growing

In pots they dance under the sun,
Taking selfies, oh what fun!
With each small sprout and leafy twist,
I find myself quite hard to resist.

Water spills and soil flies,
Sometimes I swear they have their own lies.
Whispers of leaves, gossip in green,
They giggle when I step on the scene.

Each plant a character with a face,
Some look puzzled, some find their place.
With trowels clutched like swords of yore,
We conquer weeds forevermore.

Yet every bloom brings joy, I know,
Chasing bees that buzz to and fro.
In this garden drama, I play along,
With plants that sing their joyful song.

Solstice in Bloom

The sun is shining, plants are primed,
In their little world, they're well-timed.
Sunflowers taller than my head,
Looking down like kings, I'm filled with dread.

Daisies laugh, they know the score,
While me, I stumble on the floor.
"Oh, watch your step!" the violets shout,
As I jump back, twisting about.

The greens are lush, the reds explode,
What's this new growth? A mystery code!
The garden gnomes put on a show,
Juggling veggies, oh what a flow!

It's the solstice, time to celebrate,
With carrots and laughter, it's never too late.
We dance around, with dirt on our shoes,
Living our life, we can't lose!

Harvesting Hope

With baskets ready, we hit the fields,
Veggies and dreams, our heart reveals.
Tomatoes wobble, cucumbers crawl,
Our epic quest is the best of all.

But wait! What's this? A pumpkin's grin,
Waving its leaves, where have you been?
Turnips play hide-and-seek with glee,
While carrots throw raves under their leafy tree.

Harvest time giggles, magic in hand,
We pick with glee across the land.
Mom's recipe calls for veggies galore,
But secretly, we munch on them more!

A salad's a party — that much I know,
Dressed with sunshine, watch it glow!
With laughter shared and hope in sight,
Our garden play shines oh-so-bright.

Flora's Serenade

In the quiet, petals sway and twirl,
With bees doing their happy whirl.
The daisies sing in vibrant hues,
While mint sneaks gossip, it's the latest news.

Rose bushes whisper sweet rhymes,
As I lose track of staggering times.
The lilacs plot to steal the show,
With fragrant flair that puts on a glow.

Oh, the ferns march in military fashion,
Shaking a tail in leafy passion.
And clovers cheer with a four-leaf wish,
In this whimsical world, plants really swish!

So here's to Flora and her merry crew,
In gardens alive, oh what a view!
With laughter and blooms, let spirits soar,
In this floral concert, we'll always want more!

Radiance in the Roses

Roses blush in morning sun,
Winking at the laughing bee.
Petals whisper, oh what fun!
Watch them dance, so wild and free.

Thorns are sharp, they poke with glee,
But laced with humor, they disguise.
A flower's jest, a sight to see,
As they play under azure skies.

Bees wear goggles, or so I swear,
Buzzing jokes in their tiny hives.
With pollen jokes, they charm the air,
While radiant blooms bring them high-fives.

In rose-clad fields, laughter blooms,
Each petal sings its own sweet tune.
Nature's jesters, bright as costumes,
Match the playful sun and moon.

Blossoming in Stillness

In the quiet, seeds unfold,
Tickling soil with their small dreams.
Whispers of green, stories untold,
Buds giggle as sunlight beams.

Lazily, the daisies yawn,
Stretching limbs 'til noon's parade.
Winds carry jokes across the lawn,
As flowers wink, unafraid.

The tulips sport their vibrant hats,
Ready for a garden spree.
While lazy bees in playful spats,
Buzz around, so wild and free.

A butterfly flaps, wearing shades,
With each flutter, laughter soars.
In stillness, nature's comedy cascades,
Tickling petals on lush floors.

Tinctures of Nature

Crayons burst from nature's box,
Colors clash in brilliant flair.
Flowers gossip, sneaky flocks,
Mixing shades beyond compare.

Herbs whisper recipes unheard,
Each spice, a tale from the past.
Parsley giggles, thyme's absurd,
While basil jokes, 'This won't last!'

In the breeze, a concoction brews,
Nature's elixir, pure delight.
Mint giggles as the smell ensues,
With joy that dances in the light.

Petals tumble, colors collide,
In a garden so lush, so bright.
With laughter filling every stride,
Nature's palette, purest flight.

Cloaked in Green

A leafy cloak that wraps the world,
Hiding critters with a grin.
In this forest, tales unfurled,
Jokes concoct in leafy skin.

Ferns poke fun with fronds so light,
Pranking roots beneath the ground.
Every shrub is set for flight,
Blustering laughter all around.

Vines swing low in playful jest,
Hanging on to laughter's thread.
Each branch willing to invest,
In a quip or two instead.

In green attire, nature beams,
Tickling toes of wandering feet.
Cloaked in comedy, pure dreams,
Where the fun and nature meet.

Nature's Whisper

In the garden, bees do dance,
With flowers swaying in a trance.
A daisy winks, a tulip grins,
While behind, the spinach spins.

Squirrels gossip, what a sight,
As they plan their nutty flight.
A sunflower waves, "Come, have a seat!"
While carrots shuffle on tiny feet.

Rain droplets tickle leaves above,
While chatty crickets sing of love.
A cabbage giggles, what a tease,
Yelling, "Hey, have you heard of peas?"

Nature chuckles, soft and bright,
With every bloom, a pure delight.
Let's laugh with roots, let's joke with stems,
In this garden, joy transcends.

Blossoms in the Breeze

Petals sail like little ships,
As the breeze gives gentle flips.
A daffodil does a silly spin,
While nearby, the violets grin.

Bees in bowties, oh so neat,
Sipping nectar, what a treat!
A lilac's perfume calls the bees,
"Join my dance, it's sure to please!"

A rabbit hops with so much flair,
Chasing shadows in the air.
While tulips tease with colors bold,
"Join our party, be so gold!"

In this place of bloom and jest,
Where every flower feels so blessed.
Each petal laughs in sunlight's glow,
In this garden, joy will flow.

Petal Dreams

In slumber deep, the flowers dream,
Of sunny days and a bubbling stream.
A rose hums softly, whispering tunes,
While dancing with the cheeky balloons.

Daisies topped with funky hats,
With jokes about the lazy cats.
A petunia pranks with powdery flair,
"I've hidden gnomes around somewhere!"

At night, the moon joins in the fun,
Tickling petals, one by one.
Chasing shadows, dewdrops sway,
In this night, laughter won't stray.

So sip your tea, enjoy the show,
As flowers giggle and petals glow.
In gardens bright, we dream and dare,
Join us now, if you dare!

Secrets of the Garden

In a quiet nook, the plants confide,
Sharing secrets they cannot hide.
A fern whispers tales of the past,
"Last summer's gnome? He ran so fast!"

The hydrangeas plot a splashy show,
While daisies make up wild bingo.
"I heard that tulip has a crush!"
"Oh really? Come on, let's make a hush!"

With every rustle, gossip grows,
Even rocks have stories, who knows?
The soil listens, keeping score,
In this treasure trove, there's always more!

So plant a seed and join the fun,
Where laughter sprouts in every sun.
With every bloom, a secret shared,
In this garden, laughter's bared.

Echoes of Bloom

In the garden, a gnome is in charge,
He waters the daisies with a big plastic barge.
The sunflowers giggle, they sway a bit low,
While roses tell secrets to the neighbor's crow.

Bumblebees zoom like they're late for a date,
While veggies in rows debate on their fate.
Carrots wear sunglasses, very cool indeed,
While radishes blush when the veggies take heed.

A snail's holding court on a leaf oh so wide,
While the ants dance a jig, with no place to hide.
The daisies scream, "Not today, not us!"
As the gardener trips, sending seeds in a fuss.

So here in this chaos, a riot of cheer,
Nature's a jester, the laughter we hear.
With petals in hand, let's delight in the scene,
And crown all the blooms with a laugh, quite obscene.

Sketches of Spring

Daffodils doodle on the morning dew,
While tulips on stilts sing a song or two.
A cactus in slippers attempts a ballet,
But ends up just pricking the grass on the way.

The violets gossip, they whisper with flair,
While weeds play charades in a bitter cold stare.
Forget-me-nots play hide and go seek,
And peonies' giggles make bumblebees squeak.

A worm with a mustache recites a smart rhyme,
While daisies craft plans for their next gig in mime.
"Spring has sprung, we're having a ball!"
Says a happy old fern, "Let's dance after all!"

With colors and laughter, it's quite a delight,
Nature's own circus, a whimsical sight.
In this sketch of a season, we'd all gladly play,
In gardens of humor, let's frolic away!

The Symphony of Seasons

Autumn's a joker, with leaves in a whirl,
Chasing down squirrels for a dance with a twirl.
Winter brings snowflakes, a frosty parade,
With penguins in tuxes, a grand escapade.

Spring brings the blooms, with a boisterous cheer,
As the bees form a band, buzzing tunes in the rear.
Summer's the DJ, with a sizzling mix,
As sunflowers twirl, tossing seeds like confetti tricks.

The winds of the seasons play music divine,
Each petal a note in this garden so fine.
With laughter and quirks, the flowers will sway,
In the symphony of nature, let's dance and play!

So gather your friends, let the petals perform,
Under the sun, through the wild nature's charm.
Together we thrive in this humorous show,
With seasons of fun, let our spirits just glow.

Petals on the Path

Petals on the path, a confetti parade,
As daisies make cookies, a bakery raid.
The sun tickles tulips, they giggle and sway,
While ivy rolls laughter, in its green ballet.

A butterfly flutters, all decked out in style,
Wearing a cape, oh-so-casual guile.
The herbs host a party, with flavor on hand,
While tomatoes wear hats, quite well they planned.

Along comes a breeze with a playful flick,
Carrying laughter and a hum of a trick.
The lavender whispers, "Let's have some fun!"
As the sun sets low, our pathway's begun.

So join in the dance, leave your worries behind,
In this world of petals, let your joy unwind.
With laughter aplenty, in the flowers we trust,
Let's wander this path, with humor and dust!

Murmurs from the Meadow

The daisies dance with quirky glee,
A bumblebee buzzes, "Hey, look at me!"
A dandelion shouts, "I'm a puffball star!"
While clovers play cards, 'til the sun pulls the bar.

With grass blades tickling tiny toes,
A ladybug struts, wearing tiny clothes.
A worm claims to be the wiggle champ,
As laughter erupts in the leafy camp.

The sun is a jester, making us grin,
As petals throw parties on the soft skin.
Butterflies flit with a comical flair,
In this merry green haven, laughter fills the air.

So come, take a stroll where the giggles abound,
In meadows of mirth, where joy is profound.
Each flower a friend in this silly space,
In nature's own club, we all find our place.

Petal-Powered Peace

A sunflower sighs, "It's all about me!"
While the roses giggle, drinking sweet tea.
The violets whisper, 'Let's start a show,'
With petals for curtains, and fungi for glow.

The tulips declare, "We're the tallest here!"
But short lilies laugh, 'We see all too clear.'
A dainty fern flutters with envy so mild,
As the daisies compete for the best-behaved child.

In a corner, a cactus wears shades and a grin,
"No watering needed, I'm happy within!"
While ivy climbs high on a humor-filled spree,
Yelling, "From up here, the world looks so free!"

So join in the fun, where petals unite,
In a garden of laughter and pure sheer delight.
Let's toast to the blooms, with wild and carefree,
In a petal-powered peace, just come and see!

Whispers of the Wilderness

In the forest, the ferns share secrets with trees,
"Do you think in the spring, I'll start tickling bees?"
While squirrels debate if they'll dance on a limb,
And the branches all giggle, "Aren't we all slim?"

The mushrooms hold meetings to scheme the best snacks,

While grasshoppers chatter about basic fun hacks.
"Let's leap like the rabbits, then dash to the pond!"
Then back to the bushes, where evenings abscond.

The crickets compose an enchanting, soft tune,
While the owls roll their eyes, thinking it's too soon.
A raccoon in a hat joins the band for a whirl,
In the heart of the wild, all is laughter and twirl.

So wander in wonder, let your giggles resound,
In this wilderness comedy, joy knows no bound.
Where whispers of nature craft stories so bright,
In the playful embrace of the soft starlit night.

Elysian Green

In a field of green, the llamas all prance,
Dressed in wildflowers, they twirl in a dance.
A bearded plant claims, "I'm royalty here!"
As butterflies giggle, spreading the cheer.

The moss gives out hugs to each passerby,
While frogs croak advice with a charming old sigh.
"Take life lightly!" is the mantra they chant,
In this laughter-filled realm, find your heart's recant.

Amidst joyful petals, a rabbit sings loud,
"I'm the fluffiest member of this merry crowd!"
While poppies debate who's the brightest of hue,
With every sweet blossom, more mischief ensues.

So skip through the greenery, chase every ray,
In this elysian locale, come frolic and play.
In gardens of giggles, your spirit ignites,
Where joy blooms abundantly, and every heart lights.

www.ingramcontent.com/pod-product-compliance
Lightning Source LLC
Chambersburg PA
CBHW072141200426
43209CB00051B/227